A GUY'S GUIDE

Game Face

Handling Sports On and Off the Field

ABDO
Publishing Company

A GUY'S GUIDE

Game Face

Handling Sports On and Off the Field

by Tom Robinson

Content Consultant
Dr. Robyn J. A. Silverman
Child/Teen Development Expert and Success Coach
Powerful Words Character Development

Credits

Published by ABDO Publishing Company, 8000 West 78th Street, Edina, Minnesota 55439. Copyright © 2011 by Abdo Consulting Group, Inc. International copyrights reserved in all countries. No part of this book may be reproduced in any form without written permission from the publisher. The Essential Library™ is a trademark and logo of ABDO Publishing Company.

Printed in the United States of America,
North Mankato, Minnesota
062010
092010

 THIS BOOK CONTAINS AT LEAST 10% RECYCLED MATERIALS.

Editor: Melissa Johnson
Copy Editor: Richard Reece
Interior Design and Production: Marie Tupy
Cover Design: Marie Tupy

Library of Congress Cataloging-in-Publication Data
Robinson, Tom.
  Game face : handling sports on and off the field / Tom Robinson.
    p. cm. — (Essential health : a guy's guide)
  ISBN 978-1-61613-539-3
  1. Sportsmanship—Juvenile literature. 2. Athletes—Conduct of life—Juvenile literature. I. Title. II. Title: Handling sports on and off the field.
  GV706.3.R63 2010
  175—dc22
                                    2010017073

contents

Dr. Robyn Silverman truly enjoys spending time with young people. In fact, it's what she does best! As a child and teen development specialist, Dr. Robyn has devoted her career to helping guys just like you become all they can be—and possibly more than they ever imagined. Throughout this series, you'll read her expert advice on friends, girls, classmates, school, family, and everything in between.

A self-esteem and body image expert, Dr. Robyn takes a positive approach to life. She knows how tough it is to be a kid in today's world, and she's prepared with encouragement and guidance to help you become your very best and realize your goals.

Dr. Robyn helps young people share their wildest dreams and biggest problems. Her compassion, openness, and honesty make her trusted by many adolescents, and she considers it a gift to be able to interact with the young people whom she sees as the leaders of tomorrow. She created the Powerful Words Character Development system, a program taught all over the world in martial arts and other sports programs to help guys just like you become examples to others in their communities.

As a speaker, success coach, and award-winning author, Dr. Robyn's powerful messages have reached thousands of people. Her expert advice has been featured in *Prevention* magazine, *Parenting* magazine, *U.S. News and World Report*, and the *Washington Post*. She was an expert for *The Tyra Show, Fox News,* and NBC's *LXtv.* She has an online presence, too. You can follow her on Twitter, become a fan on Facebook, and read her blog on her Web site, www.DrRobynSilverman.com. When she isn't working, Dr. Robyn enjoys spending time with her family in New Jersey.

Dr. Robyn believes that young people are assets to be developed, not problems to be fixed. As she puts it, "Guys are so much more than the way the media paints them. They have so many things to offer. I'm ready to highlight how guys get it right and tips for the ways they can make their teen years the best years so far . . . I'd be grateful if you'd come along for the ride."

When I was growing up, sports were always a big part of my life. Some of my fondest memories of childhood are games I played. But I also remember some of the sports-related problems I had to solve.

I moved to a city high school prior to my junior year. As a sophomore in the town where I was born, I played in seven varsity football games as quarterback. But it did not take long for me to realize that I had little chance of playing that position on the much stronger city team. I decided to give up football to play high school golf, where I could have more individual success.

I worked my way into the starting varsity lineup in golf. Playing as part of a team in an individual sport was not the same as playing on a football team, though. I missed that type of close teamwork. Even though I knew my place on the team would be much less significant, I returned to football for my senior year. I learned my small roles: holding for the kicker, making sure nobody got around the outside on a kickoff return, and filling in a little as a substitute in the defensive backfield. I practiced the entire season as the third quarterback, just in case of emergency, but never took another snap from center in a high school game. It did not matter. I have always been glad that I took my last opportunity to play football, regardless of what position I played.

When you play organized sports, you can experience a wide range of emotions. I hope that thinking calmly now about how to deal with some of these feelings will help you later when you face tough decisions. That way, you'll have more time and energy to enjoy the games you play.

Batter up!

Tom

1

The Tryout

Youth sports programs are designed to give everyone a fun, low-pressure introduction to new games. You get to learn about a new sport, see what it is like to be part of a team, and get some exercise. Best of all, everyone gets a chance to play.

As we get older and move up through sports, priorities slowly change. In some sports, players who show the most promise get chosen to play on special traveling or all-star teams. In other sports, you may have to go to a tryout to earn a spot on a team.

At the elementary school level, sports for younger boys are often part of gym class or an intramural program.

At the middle school or high school level, however, many sports form teams made up of the best players that compete against other schools. Terrence had already played three years of basketball in a small league at his local community center. Now that he was in middle school, he wanted to play for the school team. Check out what Terrence learned when he went to sign up.

Terrence's Story

Terrence loved basketball. He always had fun playing with his friends at the community center. He spent hours in the park shooting hoops with his brother. When Terrence heard an announcement about tryouts for the school basketball team, he decided to take a chance and go.

At the middle school or high school level, however, many sports form teams made up of the best players that compete against other schools.

Terrence went to a meeting after school to sign up. Coach Johnson wrote down everyone's name. He explained what would happen at tryouts and what was expected of players who did make the team.

"Players get three full practices to try out and show what they can do," he told the group. "Then I'll pick the players who'll be on the team for games against other schools."

Terrence didn't know what to think about the tryout. He had played basketball for three years, and last summer, for the first time, he was selected at the end of the season to play with the best players from his league in a tournament against players from other leagues. There was no tryout; Terrence's coach just told him that he was picked. So Terrence didn't feel good about going to a tryout. He figured the coach would be watching his every move, and it made him a little nervous.

Think About It

- Have you ever had to try out to be part of a team?

- How is playing on a recreational team different from being on a team that represents your school at a higher level?

- Why did Terrence feel nervous about the tryout?

During lunch at school, Terrence met some older boys who played on the middle school team. Every chance he got, he asked questions about the tryouts. How many players usually tried out? How many got to be on the team? What would they do during the tryout? He tried to picture what he was going to be asked to do. When Terrence went to the park the week before tryouts, he worked on dribbling with each hand instead of just shooting baskets.

As the day of the tryout got closer, Terrence thought about the other boys he heard were trying out. He tried to decide who was better and what his chances of making the team might be. Knowing there were older boys, too, Terrence started to worry there might not be a spot for him.

Terrence didn't feel good about going to a tryout. He figured the coach would be watching his every move, and it made him a little nervous.

One of the things Terrence had always liked about playing sports was that he made new friends, guys his own age who liked the same things he liked.

Now, instead of thinking who his new friends might be, Terrence found himself worrying about whether he was better than the other players.

Think About It

- Why does Terrence spend so much time thinking about tryouts?

- Have you ever had to compete against a friend in something you both wanted to win? Did it change the way you looked at your friend?

- Have you ever practiced something harder than usual to try to improve quickly? Did you get the results you wanted?

On the first day of tryouts, Terrence went to the gym after school and started warming up with the other guys. Coach Johnson blew his whistle, and everyone gathered around. There were 41 boys trying out, including Terrence.

Coach Johnson explained that he would keep 12 boys for the A Team of mostly seventh and eighth graders. He would keep 12 more for the B Team, which would mix boys from sixth grade, like Terrence, with some from seventh grade. That meant that only 24 out of the 41 guys trying out would make either team. Terrence looked at the guys on both sides of him. He wondered if he was better than they were.

"All right, guys," said Coach Johnson. "Time to show me what you've got!"

First, they did some dribbling drills. Terrence was really glad he'd spent extra time on his dribbling. Watching the others, he thought that he'd done well.

Next, they all took turns shooting layups. Coach Johnson was standing very near the basket, watching each move the players made. The extra scrutiny made Terrence nervous. Soon, it was his turn.

He dribbled down the line, floated the ball up . . . and it bounced off the rim. He took his second, third, fourth tries, but only made one. *Shoot!* thought Terrence. *What happened?*

The tryouts went downhill from there. Each time he made a little mistake, Terrence felt clumsier. He even dropped some simple passes that the older boys seemed to throw just a little too hard. Whenever something went wrong, Terrence looked for Coach Johnson. He always seemed to be writing something on his clipboard. Terrence wondered whether the coach was writing down what he did.

By the end of the first day, Terrence was pretty sure he wouldn't make the team. When practice ended, the coach blew his whistle and called the boys over.

"I'm sorry that I'm going to have to cut some of you in two days," Coach Johnson said. "I can tell some of you are nervous. Just try your hardest, and try not to worry. We'll see you tomorrow!"

Think About It

- Has being nervous ever made you mess something up? How did you handle your nerves? How did the situation turn out?

- How do you feel when someone is grading or evaluating you? How does it affect your performance?

When Terrence arrived the next day, he was not quite as nervous. He remembered what Coach Johnson had said and just tried as hard as he could in everything he did. Terrence noticed he played better when he was not so nervous. He noticed the other boys played well, too.

On the final day, Coach Johnson read the names of the players who made the team. Terrence did not hear his name. He would not be part of the team. The guys who made it started high-fiving and celebrating. The others started wandering back to the lockers, some upset but others looking resigned to getting cut.

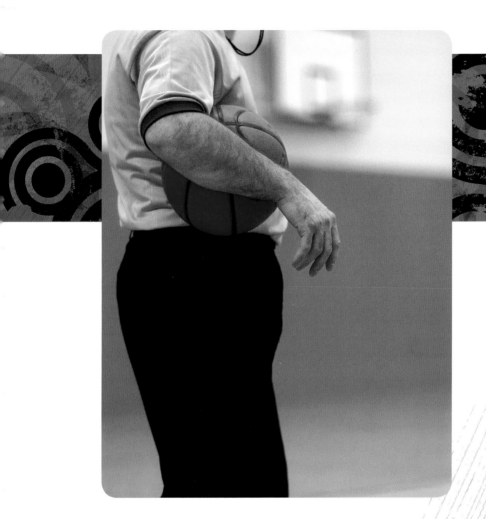

"Terrence, Sam, and Jeremy," called Coach Johnson. "Clean up, and meet me in my office."

Terrence felt a tiny bit of hope. He thought the coach must be singling him out for something special. Terrence joined Sam and Jeremy in the coach's office after they changed into their street clothes. The guys looked at each other, wondering what was happening.

"Thanks for staying, guys," said Coach Johnson. "I'm sorry you didn't make the team this year, but I saw how much effort you put in out there."

He told each boy that if he wanted to be part of the team, he could help as a scorekeeper, see what the games were like, and try again next year.

"Think about it," urged the coach, "and let me know by next week."

Terrence had to decide how much he wanted to play basketball. He could still play in the town league. The boys got together in the summer for pickup games on the outdoor courts. Would that be enough to keep him happy? Or should he put in extra time watching others play while learning about the school team and waiting for his next chance?

Think About It

- Have you ever tried out for a team or auditioned to be part of a performance?

- How did you feel when you found out you made it—or did not make it? Did you notice how others reacted to the news?

- If you were in Terrence's situation, would you be happy playing basketball elsewhere, or would you take the opportunity to be part of the school team? Why?

As you grow up, you may reach a time when an activity you always enjoyed doing for fun becomes more competitive. Maybe you always played in the band or played on a soccer team. There will most likely come a point when you are asked to try out or audition for a spot at the next level.

Tryouts can be very stressful. It's natural to be nervous. Practice might help you feel calmer. On the other hand, you might feel better if you find something completely different to do to take your mind off the tryout. Friends or family members who have been through the process could have advice for you, too. Don't be afraid to go to the coach or group leader with questions.

Not making the team can feel crushing. If this happens to you, you have a few choices. You can practice and try out again next time. You can rethink your feelings about the activity. Is it time to try a different level of competitiveness or a different activity entirely? In some cases, you might be able to get involved with the team or activity without playing. That's what Coach Johnson invited Terrence to do. Whatever you decide, put your heart into it and try your hardest.

Work It Out

1. Ask questions about the tryout process. The coach or leader is a good resource, as are friends or classmates who have been through the process already.

2. If you get wrapped up in worrying, try visualizing what steps or actions you will take to be successful. Thinking through each step may help you calm down, and it may be helpful at the tryout.

3. What if you are asked to be involved with a team without being a player? Ask the coach or leader specific questions about the actual responsibilities. Every role on the team is important.

4. Think about what is most important. Are you still staying active and picking sports you can play and enjoy your whole life?

The Last Word from Tom

If you enjoy studying a sport rather than just playing it, consider other ways to get close to the game. Offer to be a scorekeeper, statistician, or ball boy. You can learn more about what you might need to succeed in the sport on a higher level in the future. Take the opportunity to notice all the little things that contribute to a team's successes and failures.

2

Ups and Downs

There are many times in sports when an athlete's size matters. In competitions testing physical power, such as wrestling, boxing, and weight lifting, athletes are grouped against each other according to weight.

On the youth sports level, there are often restrictions in size for football to keep small players from physical mismatches against those who are much larger. These types of rules are designed to protect players. Other times, size is overemphasized in ways that can be stressful or even dangerous.

In basketball, for example, some people become obsessed with the idea that the tallest players will always win, even though that is not the case. Similarly, in football, coaches and fans sometimes pay too much attention to which team has the biggest players. See what happened to Vinnie when his coaches paid too much attention to his size.

Vinnie's Story

Vinnie was a promising young athlete. He had a growth spurt earlier than many of his friends and was used to being one of the taller and bigger guys in his grade. His size and strength got him attention in both of his favorite sports, football and wrestling.

The football season was just beginning when Coach Baum brought a few of the guys, including Vinnie, into his office after practice.

"Next year," Coach Baum said, "we'll have an open linebacker spot. I think each of you has the potential to try out for the spot next season. However, no matter how tough you are, you're not going to be able to take on those big linemen or another player who's 20 pounds heavier than you."

Coach Baum encouraged Vinnie and others to drink high-protein milk shakes while getting exercise. This way they would stay in shape but gain some weight for next season at the same time.

> The football season was just beginning when Coach Baum brought a few of the guys, including Vinnie, into his office after practice.

Vinnie started out weighing 125 pounds, and with the coach's encouragement he managed to eat enough and drink enough power milk shakes to get just above 130 pounds during the season. As the season came to an end, Coach Baum reminded him that all the starting linebackers were above 140 pounds and that he would like to see Vinnie at 145 or more when the next season started.

Think About It

- Have you ever been told that you needed to change something about yourself in order to get a position or a role you wanted? If so, what did you do?

- Do you think it was right for Coach Baum to encourage players on his team to gain weight? why or why not?

Nobody was asking Vinnie to gain weight during wrestling season. Even while he was still playing football, Vinnie would see the wrestling coach in the locker room. And the wrestling coach's advice was the opposite of the football coach's.

"The junior high wrestling team already has plenty of upper weights," explained Coach Palmer to Vinnie. "What the team really needs is some good

strong middleweights. You have the right frame for it. You can be one of those key guys if you just watch what you eat and don't get too big."

It was immediately clear when wrestling started that Coach Palmer was disappointed with Vinnie's weight. The team really needed to fill the 122-pound weight class—someone who weighed more than 115 but less than 122 pounds—and Vinnie might not be able to do that.

Coach encouraged Vinnie to get to work right away to lose those "extra pounds." Once the wrestlers were weighed before the first meet of the season, the rules limited how much weight they could lose during the season. The rules in Vinnie's state were supposed to protect wrestlers from coaches who might make them bounce up and down to different weights during the season. But the rules didn't stop coaches from trying to get wrestlers into the right weight spots before the season started.

Think About It

- Has someone who was not a doctor ever told you to gain or lose weight? What did you do?

- What could happen if Vinnie doesn't try to meet the weight the coach wants?

- Do you think the rules in Vinnie's state adequately protect athletes? Why or why not?

When wrestling season arrived, Vinnie lined up with the rest of the boys on the team before and after every practice. Each day, Coach Palmer checked their weights and filled in the numbers on a chart in the locker room. Within days, it became clear that Vinnie's weight loss was not progressing fast enough.

"Vinnie," said Coach Palmer, shaking his head, "unless you can beat out the older boys who already hold the spots at 130 and 138 pounds, you won't be part of the starting lineup."

Vinnie would only be able to wrestle in exhibitions that wouldn't be part of the team score.

"It will be a lot easier for you if you just get down to the lower class," Coach Palmer said.

Walking home after practice, Vinnie remembered feeling queasy in football season. He had made himself eat a little extra and follow it up with a protein shake, even when he did not feel like drinking one. *It's just not fair*, he thought, kicking pebbles ahead of him on the sidewalk. Just as he was getting closer to linebacker weight, he had to eat less while working out harder every day to force those pounds off before the wrestling matches started.

> Just as he was getting closer to linebacker weight, he had to eat less while working out harder every day to force those pounds off before the wrestling matches started.

Later that week, Vinnie was sitting in his afternoon social studies class. He was having trouble concentrating, and he felt sick to his stomach. When the bell rang, he stood up from his desk but sat back down heavily because his head was spinning. The teacher sent him to the nurse, who sent him home. Although he protested it was nothing, Vinnie's mom took him to the doctor.

Vinnie saw Dr. Harris, his family doctor. In reviewing what made him sick, Dr. Harris quickly zeroed in on Vinnie's eating habits.

Dr. Harris explained the situation to Vinnie and his mother. "This process of gaining and losing

weight is unhealthy for a growing boy. If Vinnie
continues to gain weight and then diet, he could
suffer serious medical consequences in the future."

Dr. Harris sent a letter to the school stating that, for medical reasons, Vinnie was not allowed to try to get his body weight below 130 pounds.

At first, Vinnie was relieved. The doctor's letter would keep the wrestling coach from pressuring him. But, as he thought about it, Vinnie wondered how the season would go. *Will I even get a spot in the lineup?* he worried. *Will Coach Palmer be mad?* And Vinnie realized he could have the opposite problem when football season came around and the pressure to bulk up would start again.

will I even get a spot in the lineup? he worried. will Coach Palmer be mad?

Think About It

- Have you ever felt like you let down a coach or other role model when you were not able to accomplish something he or she wanted? If so, how did you handle the situation?

- Do you think Vinnie will be happier if he has a less important spot on the wrestling team but does not have to face the pressures of losing weight?

Doctors often guide their patients to lose, maintain, or gain weight for health or medical reasons. Manipulating body weight to fit a sports weight category, however, can create unnecessary risks. Even weight gain and loss for medical reasons is usually healthiest when handled gradually.

Aiming for a specific number on the scale can encourage dangerous practices. Healthful habits, including exercising and eating a balanced diet, should help the body settle at its ideal weight. It is important to practice good habits to move toward a healthier weight rather than aiming at a predetermined weight and working to hit that goal.

Forcing weight loss in a physically fit athlete when the body is growing naturally is particularly unsafe. Any significant change of body weight or diet should be pursued only with a doctor's guidance.

Work It Out

1. If you believe you need to gain or lose weight, ask your doctor for a medical opinion and for help creating a healthy eating and exercise plan.

2. Any body change is safest when it happens gradually. Avoid supplements or diets that promise quick results without work—they generally are not designed for young people who are still growing, and they can be dangerous.

3. If you are feeling pressured by a coach to gain or lose weight, talk to your parents or another trusted adult. They will help you find a balanced, healthy approach to meet your goals, or they will help you stay out of a dangerous, unhealthy situation.

The Last Word from Tom

In sports, individuals are often asked to make sacrifices for the good of the team. At no point, however, should those sacrifices involve doing something that is unsafe or unhealthy. If you feel you are being encouraged to do something unsafe, it is important to discuss it with a parent or other adult you trust. Seek advice on any situation in which you feel uncomfortable. In sensitive situations, have your parent or a trusted adult join you for a meeting with the coach.

3

Show Time

Sometimes sports seem to be as much about putting on a show as they are about determining who wins or loses. On a higher level, where the reaction of a large crowd becomes part of the game's atmosphere, there are many examples of players taking showboating too far. Professional and college sports have added many rules to control celebrations that embarrass or show up opponents.

It is natural to want to celebrate a successful accomplishment with teammates. It makes sense to congratulate each other. It is good to acknowledge that the effort of the group made your team successful. Celebrating

goes too far, however, if one player draws too much attention to himself or makes fun of a player on the other side.

Both losing and winning carry responsibilities. A good loser deals with disappointment in a mature way. A good winner shows respect for a worthy effort by an opponent. Will Joey learn what it takes to be a good winner?

Celebrating goes too far, however, if one player draws too much attention to himself or makes fun of a player on the other side.

Joey's Story

Joey stood far away from the line of scrimmage, ready to defend one last fourth-down pass with ten seconds to go. He knew that North was in position to win the football game. As the receivers charged off the line toward him, Joey backed up farther, getting closer to the goal line. He was surprised to see the high pass floating right to him as if he were fielding a punt.

The ball was thrown too far for any of the receivers, and Joey easily made the interception. He took off, angling toward his own bench with room to run and time to see that the clock was ticking off the last couple of seconds. He could hear his teammates cheering from the sideline. As long as Joey didn't fumble before going to the ground or running out of bounds, North would win.

Joey turned and ran straight toward the sideline. A Valley receiver chased desperately after him. Just as he reached and stepped over the sideline to end the play, Joey waved the ball at the player chasing him, teasing him with the ball held just out of reach.

Joey thought he was safe on the sideline, when suddenly he got slammed to the ground. Now, the cheering turned to yelling as the referee pulled the receiver off Joey. The referee and the Valley coaches scolded the other player for losing his cool and making an unnecessary hit.

Think About It

- How do you think Joey felt as he ran toward the sideline watching the clock run out? What was he thinking?

- Were Joey's actions a celebration of winning or a taunt directed at a losing opponent?

- What do you think the Valley receiver was thinking as he chased Joey? How would he have felt when he saw Joey tease him with the ball?

Win or lose, Joey and his father always stopped for a snack or a shake and had a quick talk about the game before heading home. This time, however, Joey's dad drove straight for home. With the car parked in the driveway, Joey's dad turned to talk to his son.

"Joey, do you know why we didn't stop this time?" he asked.

"Not really. Why?" replied Joey.

"We usually stop after games because I am proud watching you play, and I enjoy talking about the game with you afterward."

Joey's dad explained that he was disappointed that Joey would taunt another player and show off.

"Joey, you've been on the losing team. How would you feel if a guy on the other team starts taunting you when the game is basically over?"

"I guess I wouldn't like it," Joey answered, looking down at his hands.

Think About It

- Why did Joey's father change their postgame routine?

- What could Joey have done to show he was a good sport after the interception?

- Did Joey's father discuss the situation with him in the right way?

Joey felt ashamed and upset. He went out back and started shooting baskets in the hoop up above the garage door. Working up a sweat helped clear his thoughts.

He knew he wanted his dad to be proud of him again. Thinking back, he knew his dad cheered just as hard whether he won or lost the game. The only time his dad wasn't proud was when he was a poor sport. Joey knew he'd have to figure out the line between celebrating and being mean. After all, the guys on the other team were trying their hardest, too. He knew he would not want to have it rubbed in his face when he came up short in a game, either.

Think About It

- Think about your actions in successful game situations. Have you ever made fun of an opponent?

- How would you expect the winning team to act when you have just lost a close game?

- Have you ever done something physical to help work out your thoughts or problems? Did the exercise help you feel better?

Observers often come away from a sporting event impressed by the accomplishments of the winning team. The good impression can be ruined, though, if a team or player is unable to win with dignity. Poor sportsmanship in the form of taunting or disrespecting opponents spoils a team's image.

Playing sports is a great way to learn about respecting others' feelings. Remember that there are many ways to celebrate the success of your team without doing things that are designed to make others feel bad. Winning without gloating and losing without complaining is a way to protect the spirit of the game. When we protect the spirit of the game, everyone has fun.

Work It Out

1. Watch college or professional level sports and pay attention to how the players celebrate. Discuss with your family or friends which actions you see are positive and which are negative.

2. As you prepare to play, consider how your actions might affect others' feelings. Be aware of the image you create for yourself. Think about how you would feel if someone on the other team performed the same action.

3. Practice good sportsmanship by congratulating the other team whether you win or lose. Always show others that you have strong values and honor them no matter what the outcome.

4. Become a positive leader for good sportsmanship on your team. Watch how your team and coach respond to you.

The Last Word from Tom

Achievements in sports are the result of practicing proper techniques. Good sportsmanship is like any other skill you bring to your sport. Prepare yourself for reacting to success and failure just as you practice the actions you will need to perform in competition. Away from the field, take some time to think about how you have reacted and how you want to react to both success and failure. Having a plan in place will help you to deal with either one in the right way.

4

Playing for Dad

Many people's first sports memories involve their families. Maybe you've been cheering for your mom's team since before you remember. A family member may have been the person who showed you how to swing a bat, kick a soccer ball, or shoot a foul shot. A parent might have signed you up for a sports team for the first time.

Our parents share sports with us when they make time to take us to practice and come to watch our games. Most of the time, parents are supportive as they watch their children learn the games they remember playing themselves.

There are times, however, when parents can lose perspective. The excitement of watching their children play causes some parents to have unrealistic expectations. Parents might forget that the game is supposed to be fun. Some parents might use their children's games to relive their own playing days. Others might push their children to accomplish the things they never did. This was the situation in which Malik found himself.

Malik's Story

Malik's dad, Omar, was always reminding him how lucky he was. "You have so many chances to play sports," he would say. "I never had that when I was a kid." Omar had lived in a very small town, and Little League baseball was the only game he got to play in an organized league. When Omar moved to a bigger city at age 12, all the other kids were already better at basketball, football, soccer, and any other game he tried. "I probably could've been really good in high school," Omar told Malik, "if I'd had all the chances you do."

Omar made sure Malik never took a break. He wanted Malik to try every sport while he was young, so he could play on any team he wanted when he got

> *The excitement of watching their children play causes some parents to have unrealistic expectations. Parents might forget that the game is supposed to be fun.*

to high school. When baseball ended, soccer started. When soccer ended, basketball started. During basketball, Omar signed up Malik for a wrestling club to see how he would do there. On summer weekends, they played golf together. Omar sent Malik to youth golf tournaments in the morning, sometimes on the same days he had baseball games in the afternoon.

Think About It

- why do you think it is important to Omar that Malik get as many chances to play sports as possible?

- Do you play several sports? How do sports fit in with your other activities?

Malik liked playing golf with his dad, but he never did well in the tournaments. Omar kept telling him how good he would be in every sport in high school, but Malik was just an average player on most of his teams. He did not get nearly as excited as his dad seemed to when he thought about playing in the future. What made his dad so sure things would be different in the years ahead?

Think About It

- Why might Malik do better playing golf with his father than playing in tournaments?

- Is Malik's father being realistic about Malik's future in sports?

Malik struggled through an exhausting June. All the competitions were ruining his summer. He knew it would only be worse once the school year started and he would have to balance homework and practices again. His dad wanted him to play so badly, though, that Malik couldn't bring himself to say anything. He didn't want to disappoint his dad.

One night after a late dinner following a golf tournament and an afternoon baseball game, Malik

went back into the kitchen quietly. His parents were doing dishes, and they were talking about him.

"Malik seems tired and unhappy," said his mom. "I think he needs to quit one of his sports so he has more free time."

"Malik doesn't appreciate all the opportunities he's getting. His new fitted clubs and those nice courses he plays on are expensive. He needs to do a better job, or else he's wasting all the money I spent."

"Omar!" said Malik's mom. "Are you saying that spending time with your son is a waste?"

She turned her head and noticed Malik lingering in the doorway. "Malik, come in here. I'm worried that you're unhappy. Do you want to stay on all your teams?"

"Dad," said Malik tentatively. "I love golfing with you. I just spend all my time practicing or competing. I need time to do other things, too."

"But you have all these opportunities—"

"Yes," inserted his mom, "opportunities. Not obligations."

"I want sports to be fun again," explained Malik, finally looking his dad in the eyes. "When *"If I could concentrate on one or two, I'd work really hard and maybe get better."* I'm jumping from sport to sport, I stop liking any of them. If I could concentrate on one or two, I'd work really hard and maybe get better. It would be more fun for me."

Omar finally heard what his son was saying. "If this is really what you want," he said. "I only want what's best for you."

Think About It

- Why do you think Malik's father made an issue about the money he has spent?

- Do you think Malik will enjoy sports more if he cuts back?

- How can Malik choose which sports to continue pursuing and which to give up?

Many parents want to create better opportunities for their children than what they had when they were younger. Some parents want their children to live in a nicer house and get a better education than they did, for example. This desire can also carry over to other issues such as sports and other activities a parent feels he or she missed out on.

Generally, your parents only have the best intentions. But sometimes they do not realize that their desires don't match up with yours. If your parents are pressuring you to participate in an activity that you don't enjoy, try to talk to them about it. Ask why they want you to participate and what they hope you will get out of it. Explain to them why you don't want to participate anymore. If they don't agree with your point of view right away, offer to work out a compromise. Let them know what you would rather do instead. If the pressure gets really bad or your parents won't listen to your reasons, consider seeking help from a counselor or another adult you trust.

Work It Out

1. Once you have tried several different sports, think about the positives and the negatives of being involved in each one. Make sure you are participating for the right reasons. Discuss your decision and your reasoning with your parents.

2. Don't let one incident make you decide to quit something too quickly.

3. If you decide to cut back on activities, think carefully about which ones you are likely to continue to enjoy and which ones you are unlikely to miss.

4. Is there an alternative that might allow you to still play a sport with less time commitment? In Malik's case, this could be playing golf for fun but not in competition.

The Last Word from Tom

Your parents' desires might put unnecessary pressure on you. They almost never mean to do it, though. They're just trying to do what's best for you. Try to understand and appreciate what your parents are trying to do. Be sure to thank them. That should help make it easier to talk to them when something's not working out for you.

5

Peak Performance

Many sports combine teamwork, strategy, and playing ability. Most sports competition also involves some use of strength or speed. Many sports combine both. Practice and hard work can improve your personal performance—but only to a certain point.

The news is full of examples of professional and Olympic-level athletes who have taken shortcuts to getting bigger, stronger, and faster. People take performance-enhancing drugs because they may find that drugs improve their athletics in the short term. However, the drugs endanger a person's mental and physical well-being.

Using most performance-enhancing drugs means breaking the rules of the game and breaking the law, too. Dominick found out why others have felt the temptation to gain an edge in competition.

Dominick's Story

Dominick had always been one of the best football players on his team, but now that the high school coach wanted him to go right from the eighth grade team to varsity in his freshman year, he had a problem. The high school team got together three times every week in the winter for weight lifting to get ready for the next season.

When Dominick got to the weight room, he realized that although he was bigger than most eighth graders, he was one of the smallest guys in the room. He positioned himself on the bench press machine after one of the sophomore players left and could not budge the bar. He had to take some of the weight off before beginning his lift.

When the amount of weight each player lifted was written up on the charts on the wall, Dominick saw proof that he was also not as strong as most of the other players. He started to worry about joining them on the field in the coming months.

He positioned himself on the bench press machine after one of the sophomore players left and could not budge the bar.

Think About It

- How does Dominick feel when he thinks about playing varsity football next fall? How would you feel in his position?

- Is it important for Dominick to be as big and strong as the other boys when the season starts? If so, what can he do about it? What changes are beyond his control?

Casey, a junior lineman and one of the strongest players on the team, noticed Dominick staring at the charts almost every day. After a few weeks, Casey decided to have a chat with Dominick.

"I can let you in on a little secret," Casey said as he walked up to Dominick, who was standing in front of the board where the totals were listed. "Those numbers go up faster if you're willing to do what it takes," Casey said.

"I just want to be able to play," Dominick said. "I'll do whatever it takes."

"Are you sure you mean that?"

The way Casey was looking at him made Dominick a little nervous, but he nodded.

"You already take supplements, right?"

Dominick nodded again.

"Well, I can get you something that works even faster. You wanna make the team, right?"

Dominick knew Casey was talking about steroids. He didn't know what to think. He had heard that steroids were dangerous, but he had also heard stories about many successful professional athletes who were accused of using them. Dominick thought it was possible steroids might help him. He wondered if taking them for just a little while might help him catch up to the older players.

"Yeah, maybe," Dominick replied. "I gotta think it over."

Think About It

- Have you ever been in a position to try to compete with guys older than you?

- What impact do age and strength differences make on playing a sport?

Later that week, Casey approached Dominick in the weight room again.

"Have you thought about it?" Casey asked. "I get the stuff for the other guys. I could get some for you, too."

Dominick must have looked unsure. Casey leaned in closer, almost whispering. "Everybody says they're dangerous just because they don't want some guys to get ahead. If they were that dangerous, nobody would use them," Casey said persuasively. "How do you think all these guys got so strong?"

The side effects Dominick read about on posters in the locker room, however, made it sound scary. He still wasn't sure, but he didn't want Casey to take back his offer, either.

"Lemme see how much money I have, okay? I'll tell you in a few days," he said to Casey, walking out of the gym.

On his walk home, Dominick kept thinking about Casey's offer. He wondered if people would be able to tell, if he would look different enough that people would notice. Would it be cheating? Where would he get the money to pay for them? What if he got caught with the steroids? Would he go to jail?

For every reason Dominick could think of to just stay away from drugs, he kept returning to one problem. *How can I compete if everyone else is taking steroids and I'm not?*

That night, Dominick couldn't sleep. The idea of getting to be part of the varsity team at such a young age wasn't as appealing as it was before. Dominick didn't know what to do. He hated how complicated everything was. He wished he could just play football.

Think About It

- How could Dominick find out more about the health risks involved with performance-enhancing drugs?

- What could happen if Dominick decides to take steroids?

- What other factors, besides health, should be part of Dominick's decision?

Many athletes who take performance-enhancing drugs see positive results before any serious problems appear. However, this does not mean the danger has passed. Some of the long-term effects of unprescribed anabolic steroids include mood swings, trembling, heart damage, urinary problems, and even death. In men, steroids can also cause acne, breast growth, testicle shrinkage, and erectile dysfunction.

You also cannot assume that currently legal supplements are safe—especially for a growing guy. Many guys believe supplements are okay just because they are available. However, many substances that were once legal were later found to be dangerous. In addition, a safe substance can become dangerous if too much is taken. Overdosing on any drug-related product is typically unhealthy.

While many guys are trying to keep up by taking performance-enhancing drugs or over-the-counter supplements, they may just be cheating themselves. What seems like a shortcut today can lead to long-term problems tomorrow.

Work It Out

1. Educate yourself about supplements and performance-enhancing drugs and their side effects.

2. "Getting an edge" can be another way to say "cheating." It might seem as though everyone else is doing it—but that doesn't make it right.

3. Try to keep sports in perspective. Getting ahead by taking banned or dangerous substances is not worth the consequences.

The Last Word from Tom

One of the challenges in sports is finding a way to keep improving your performance. The feeling of satisfaction you get as you improve your skills is a major reason why many people play sports. Improving through cheating takes away that satisfaction.

Health risks alone should provide enough reasons to avoid performance-enhancing drugs. But there are other consequences. Those who take drugs have to live with the fear of being caught. They know they can lose it all—even more quickly than steroids gave it to them.

6

Voice in the Crowd

Having your parents at the game is really important for many guys. Hearing your family cheering you on can give you that extra motivation to get the run or the touchdown.

Some parents, however, get too wrapped up in the game. If a parent starts yelling at the refs, coaches, or other players, they've crossed the line. Reports from across the country tell of incidents that have even involved physical violence. Fighting among parents or assaults on coaches and game officials are extreme examples, but any time the actions of parents and spectators distract attention from the playing field to the sidelines, it's wrong. See how Victor faced such a situation.

Victor's Story

When Victor was nine, he complained to his dad that the youth soccer coach was making the players run too much at practice. Some of the other kids and parents were upset, but only Victor's dad, Steven, spoke up. The other parents said they were afraid of what would happen to their kids if they complained, but Steven addressed the concern with the coaches and wound up speaking out at a league meeting. In the end, the officials agreed with Victor's dad that the running had become too extreme. Victor was proud of his dad.

> *Some parents, however, get too wrapped up in the game. If a parent starts yelling at the refs, coaches, or other players, they've crossed the line.*

Sometimes, though, Victor didn't appreciate it as much when his dad spoke up at sporting events. When the umpire in the Little League play-off game seemed to call every pitch against his team, other parents grumbled, but Steven came to the fence and yelled at the umpire for everyone to hear.

Victor and his teammate Ronnie both struck out when the umpire called the third strike on pitches near their knees. When their pitcher was on the mound with the bases loaded, the call went the

other way. "Where was that?" Steven yelled. The umpire didn't look but made a little motion with his hand to show that it was too low. "You called those pitches strikes when we batted," Steven argued. "That's the same pitch. You have to call it the same way."

Some fans agreed. Others were getting uncomfortable as they listened to the argument.

Steven even tried to convince the umpire to come to the fence so he could talk to him between innings.

Soon, Victor realized that his dad seemed to be yelling at someone at every game. Sometimes he was mean about it. At other times, he tried making funny comments, but only a few people laughed. Victor could even hear his coaches talking about it.

Think About It

- How should a parent act publicly if he or she thinks his or her son is not being treated fairly at a game or practice?
- why did Victor think his father's involvement was a good thing at first?
- what is making Victor start to change his mind?

The baseball season ended without anything worse happening, and soccer began. Victor's dad started making comments and yelling even at the first game. Victor was so distracted he missed a couple of easy passes and kicked the ball wide of the net when he could have scored an easy goal.

In the car on the way home, Victor's dad asked, "What happened out there? The goalie was miles away and your kick was nowhere near the net. Where was your head?"

Victor couldn't take it anymore. "It's all your fault!" he yelled. "You can't keep your big mouth shut and you distracted me!"

"I distracted you?" replied Steven indignantly. "You've gotta be able to play through much worse than that!"

"I hate it when you come to my games," shot back Victor. "You're the guy in the stands everyone wants to shut up."

"Huh," Steven let his breath out. "What do you want me to do, ignore the ref's mistakes?"

"They're not mistakes. Look, would you please just be quieter?"

"Fine, I'll try to let things slide. But you've gotta bring your game up!"

The two sat in silence for the rest of the ride.

Think About It

- Do you expect Victor's dad to be quieter now?

- Have you been at games when one fan is louder and more negative than the rest? What do you think about that person?

Steven was on his best behavior for a couple of soccer games, but after a little while he stopped controlling himself. He didn't yell at officials

anymore, though—he just developed a new habit. When Victor collided with someone on the other team, he'd hear, "That was a cheap shot. You'd better watch what you're doing, number 12."

When Steven wasn't calling out opponents, he turned his attention to Victor's teammates. "Victor's open!" he shouted. "Stop dribbling with your head down. Pass the ball sometimes!"

Other parents got angry with Steven for yelling at their sons. Sometimes, other parents yelled back at Steven. The players on the field could no longer hear cheers of encouragement over the arguments going on among the spectators.

Finally, some parents spoke to league officials. Victor's dad—and anyone else who acted inappropriately—was banned from games for the rest of the season.

Steven complained to some of the other parents, but he got little sympathy. Everyone told him he was being a poor sport and that what he was doing only made things harder on his son. Victor was embarrassed and hoped his dad would stop overreacting. He wondered what would happen when basketball started up.

Think About It

- Have you seen adults acting inappropriately at youth or school sporting events? Did anyone do anything to stop the situation?

- Do you think there should be rules regarding parents' conduct at youth sporting events?

- Did you ever wish you could play organized games with other kids without adults watching?

There is nothing wrong with a parent asking a coach or an official respectful questions about the game. Sometimes there is a true problem with the way a game is being handled, and a parent's actions can help correct it. A parent's actions are inappropriate, however, if they interfere with the game in any way. If your parent is out of control at your games, the first step is to talk to him or her about it. Explain how his or her actions make you feel, and what he or she can do to help you feel better. You may also try asking other family members or your coach for help with the situation.

What if your parent doesn't stop after you've talked about it? Talk to your school counselor or another adult you trust. If the situation is bad enough, a coach or league official might take actions to stop your parent's disruptive behavior.

An important reason to address spectator issues is because spectators can really make a difference in a game. A 2009 research study showed that when spectators were negative, players reflected that negativity. When spectators were more positive, players behaved more positively.

Work It Out

1. If any written material is sent home regarding expectations or conduct for players or their parents, make sure the whole family reads it.

2. If your league or team conducts parents' meetings, encourage your parents to go.

3. If a parent is doing something at games that makes you uncomfortable, tell your parent how hard it is for you to focus on the game and have fun when all that other stuff is going on.

The Last Word from Tom

Your parents will always want to stand up for you. Sometimes, though, they can cross the line and overreact when you wish they wouldn't. Ninety-nine percent of the time, talking to them will fix the problem. Whatever your parents do, remember that their behavior is not your fault. You can only control your own actions.

Great Expectations

Sometimes athletic talent doesn't run in families. If your father was the star quarterback when he was in high school, it's not necessarily true that you can throw a tight spiral down the field. Your older sister might have been the best blocker on her volleyball team—but maybe your best "sport" is chess.

It's hard enough for someone who likes sports to feel as if he has to measure up to past successes. If you don't really like sports, it's even worse. When a parent or an older sibling was really good at his or her sport, family and friends may still talk about it. Some people might ask why you don't have the same

talents or interests. You may be pushed into doing things you don't want to do just to live up to others' expectations. Brendan felt that kind of pressure all the time.

Brendan's Story

Brendan was always surprised at how many people remembered his mother when he visited with his grandparents in her old hometown. During lunch at the town restaurant, a few extra

It's hard enough for someone who likes sports to feel as if he has to measure up to past successes. If you don't really like sports, it's even worse.

visitors would always stop by the table to say hello and tell Brendan how much he looked like his mom when she was his age and tell stories from when she was in high school.

Brendan had heard them so many times that he could practically recite the stories himself: how the tall, skinny girl from the small town had finished first in the entire state in the high jump in high school, and how she got half of her college paid for with a basketball scholarship. The pictures in his mom's old school yearbooks all seemed to show her with a medal around her neck or receiving another award.

The stories were not as much fun as they used to be. Now those visitors asked about Brendan's sports and whether he was "just as big of a star as his mom." When she was with him, she always said, "Of course he is," even though they both knew it wasn't true. When old friends talked to his mom, Brendan just wished he could be somewhere else.

Think About It

- How do you think Brendan felt when he first heard the stories about his mom? How do you think he feels now?

- Have you ever played a sport that a parent or other older relative was good at? Did their success make playing the sport easier or more difficult?

- Why do you think Brendan's mom says he is better at sports than he actually is?

Brendan knew he would never be one of the better players. He began to wonder if his mom was ashamed to admit it to her old friends.

On the car ride home, Brendan's mom noticed that he was unusually silent.

"Honey, what's wrong?" she asked. "You're really quiet today."

"Nothing. I don't want to talk about it."

"No, tell me," she pushed.

"Why do you tell your friends I'm good at sports like you were? Why don't you just tell the truth?" he asked. "I stink."

"Oh, honey, you don't stink!"

She started thinking back. "I had so much fun back then. I loved competing, and I spent every spare moment at practice or doing extra running. I had to work really hard to be as good as I was—but I really loved doing it."

Brendan knew he would never be one of the better players.

She paused for a moment. "That was a different time and place," she said. "It's easier to stand out in a small town."

This didn't make Brendan feel any better. Now, he had different questions about what his mom really thought. *Is she trying to say I don't work hard enough at sports?* No matter which way he looked at it, Brendan came back to the same point. His lack of success seemed to be a disappointment to his mother.

Think About It

- Do you ever think you have to participate in activities just because your parents did when they were your age?

- Do you think it bothers Brendan's mom that he is not as successful in sports as she was when she was his age?

On his walk home from school later in the week, Brendan could not stop thinking about his mother's comments about hard work. *What exactly did she mean?* He thought it might be true that he wasn't the hardest worker on his team. But he also didn't think it was fair to assume he never worked hard, either.

Brendan spent the rest of the day stewing over his mom's comments about hard work. He kept his feelings pent up, saying nothing at dinner and just pushing his food around on his plate.

His mom noticed his lack of appetite. "Brendan, why aren't you eating?" she asked.

Brendan couldn't keep his feelings in any longer. He slammed his fork on the table. "Why do you think I'm a slacker?" he burst out.

"Have I ever called you a slacker?" she asked, looking puzzled.

"When you were talking about how hard you had to work to be so good, and how much you loved practice and doing extra running and stuff."

"I didn't mean to say that you—" she started.

"Well I do work hard!" Brendan interrupted. "I get great grades in science because it's really interesting and I like doing extra research. Sports are okay, but I'm never going to be as good as you were, and lots of times I'd rather be working on a science project."

"If you don't enjoy sports, I'm certainly not going to make you stay on a team," his mom said. "I'm sorry. I never knew those old stories made you feel bad. I only want you to be happy and spend time doing things that are exciting to you! If that's science—then that's great."

She patted his shoulder and smiled. "Now, tell me about your project so I can brag about you to my friends next time we go to Grandma's."

Think About It

- Do you think Brendan understood his mother's comments about hard work correctly?

- Do you think Brendan should try harder to be better in sports?

- At what activity or subject do you work the hardest? Do other people notice how hard you work?

In general, we are proud of our family members' accomplishments. It's special to know that your mom won state, or your dad played college hoops, and that everyone still remembers how great they were. It's tough, though, if it seems like everyone expects you to repeat their successes or love the same activities they did when growing up. As much as our parents shape who we are, we do not share all of the same interests and abilities. You may feel pressure to follow in your parents' footsteps, but you need to live your own life, too.

It's important to try different activities. You can figure out what you are good at and what you love doing. Don't worry about being different from your parents or siblings. After all, you are your own person. If you are feeling pressure to excel at an activity you don't care for, talk to your family about it. Tell them about what you're really interested in and what new things you'd like to try. Your family members want you to succeed at something you love to do.

Work It Out

1. When you were younger, your parents probably chose many activities for you.

Now that you are older, you have more freedom to choose activities for yourself. Be on the lookout for things you want to try and tell your parents about them.

2. Once you have started participating in an activity, rethink from time to time if it is something you want to continue doing. Just because you played soccer for three years doesn't mean you have to keep playing it if you aren't interested in it anymore.

3. It can be hard to grow if you feel as though you are standing in someone else's shadow. You have talents and interests of your own—find something you love doing. If you are losing your self-confidence, however, talking to a counselor or an adult you trust may help you feel better about yourself.

The Last Word from Tom

We may be very similar to our parents, but each person still has his or her own wants and needs. Many people are happy following in the footsteps of older family members, but not everyone is. You don't have to feel trapped by what others have done before you. What is best for you now may be entirely different than what worked for them.

8

Bench Support

Whether through natural talent or hard work, some athletes on any given team will be better than others. It is expected that teammates of different skill levels will still play together as a team, however. People with different talents often perform different roles on the team, too. Every star quarterback has to have protection, after all.

The problems begin when people start treating the stars better than other players. It's easy to focus on the star, but a team can get into trouble if it forgets that it needs all of its members to succeed. Dwayne and his team, the Tigers, found this out the hard way.

Dwayne's Story

Dwayne was rough on his less-skilled teammates. He called it "garbage time" when the coach played more backups, and he did not try hard if he had to be out there with the substitute players on the junior high basketball team. When one of Dwayne's fancy, no-look passes went through Brad's hands and smacked him in the face, Dwayne did not bother to see if his teammate was okay. Instead, he just ran by and said, "Don't worry, I won't ever try passing you the ball again."

The problems begin when people start treating the stars better than other players. It's easy to focus on the star, but a team can get into trouble if it forgets that it needs all of its members to succeed.

Dwayne's natural talent made everything look easy, and he was clearly the best player on the team. He thought it was a waste of time to play with guys who weren't as good as he was. He often went to the other end of the gym to shoot free throws and layups by himself when the coach wanted him to help out a teammate. When he did help out, he made nasty comments the whole time. After a particularly bad practice, Coach Matthews called Dwayne aside.

"Dwayne, your attitude's been pretty bad lately. Basketball is a team game. You have to be willing to work with everyone. You've gotta shape up, or I've got some serious concerns about you staying on the team."

"Right, coach," replied Dwayne. He smiled, though inside he was angry. *Coach doesn't see how much work I do, pulling those losers along*, he thought. *Well, I'll work with them—and show him how much they stink!*

After that, Dwayne worked with the subs. However, he did everything he could to make them look bad, passing the ball too hard or making snide comments under his breath so his teammates could hear but the coach couldn't. Before long, every guy who stayed on the bench had come to dread working with Dwayne.

Think About It

- How should teammates treat each other? Do you think Dwayne's actions were acceptable?

- How do the more-skilled players treat the less-skilled players on your teams?

- Have your coaches spent time teaching you how to work together as a team? Should they be teaching that?

As the basketball play-offs approached, Dwayne's team lost one starter when Steven sprained his ankle. Another, Ian, was home with strep throat when the play-offs started. Dwayne was used to

scoring points and winning games. He expected his team to win the championship. But when Shareek and Malcolm got into foul trouble and fouled out of the semifinal game, everything changed.

Timmy and Jon, usually the last two players to get in most games, shared one of the spots during the first half. There were times late in the game when both had to play. The other backups were a little more experienced than Timmy and Jon were, but not by much.

The other team quickly realized Dwayne was the best at dribbling and passing, as well as the only player comfortable shooting the ball. With the other starters out of the Tigers lineup, the Warriors' defense put extra attention on stopping Dwayne. The Warriors were able to keep two guards on Dwayne for most of the rest of the game.

When Dwayne got stuck and had to pass the ball, he looked around the court at his teammates. Timmy was unguarded and in a good position to shoot if he got the ball.

Dwayne thought Timmy looked really nervous. He thought Timmy would probably drop the pass, so he threw the ball toward another teammate instead. A Warrior player snagged the pass, though, and took it down for an easy layup.

Think About It

- what can the better players do to make others feel more comfortable?

- why was Timmy nervous?

The Tigers' early lead slipped away. With the game tied and only two minutes left, Dwayne was trapped again. He had to pass, but none of his teammates seemed to know where he was looking. He passed to Jon—who turned the other way and missed the ball, which went bouncing out of bounds.

Dwayne blocked a Warrior shot and got the ball back, but he wasn't close enough to shoot when he needed to pass again. He threw to Timmy, but his pass was stolen. The Warriors took it back for another layup to break the tie with 40 seconds left.

The substitute players tried the best they could. Even Dwayne could see that. They played hard on defense and fought for rebounds, but they were nervous playing offense, especially when Dwayne had the ball. Timmy dove on the floor to save the ball once, and Jon wrestled with one of the Warriors to fight for a rebound. On the other end, the Warriors

didn't let Dwayne take anything but desperate off-balance shots. He could not hit them, and his team did not score for what turned out to be the last five minutes of their season. Even with good defense, they lost 37–34.

Seeing how hard they tried, Dwayne knew that just a little work on some parts of their game would have enabled his teammates to pull out the win. If they had just gotten past the Warriors, Ian, Shareek, and Malcolm would have been back in the next game. The Tigers might have won the championship. As Dwayne changed in the locker room, he thought about the "garbage time" when he didn't try his hardest. He realized that if they had learned to play together earlier in the season, it would have helped the team in the end.

Walking out, he spotted Timmy on the way to his car with his parents.

"Wait up!" called Dwayne, speeding up to catch his teammate.

Timmy stopped, surprised that Dwayne was talking to him.

"Timmy, you worked your butt off out there tonight."

Timmy looked startled, and then smiled slowly. "Thanks, I think."

"Want to play some pickup next weekend?" added Dwayne. "We can work on passing some more."

Timmy smiled wider. "Yeah, that'd be great. See ya tomorrow."

Dwayne was already excited for next year.

Think About It

- Was it reasonable to expect the substitute players to be ready when needed?
- What can Dwayne do next time to help his teammates prepare for a big game?

Teams are naturally going to be made up of players with different sets of skills and various levels of ability. Every player on the team is important. More-skilled players should try to help teammates who struggle. All coaches and players should share one important goal: to help each individual member and the team as a whole improve throughout the season.

A player who is already struggling to keep up will have even more trouble if he is nervous about being accepted by teammates. When a skilled player takes the time to encourage his younger or less-skilled teammates, he sets an example that is likely to be followed by the entire team. Instead of being frustrated by the limitations of some players, you should try to make those players more comfortable and help them to identify their strengths.

If you are one of the younger or less experienced players and your teammates make you nervous, start by talking privately with your coach. If you're uncomfortable, it's not good for the team, and your coach will probably take steps to address the situation.

Work It Out

1. While learning new skills at the beginning of a sports season, also pay attention to how your teammates play. See which teammates you can learn from, and also whom you might be able to help out.

2. Try to develop ways teammates can help each other during games.

3. If you think some players on your team are not being treated fairly, talk to your coach about it. If you think your coach is part of the problem, ask your parents to help you talk to your school or league about possible solutions.

The Last Word from Tom

Team building is an important part of sports. Every member of a team has an important role to fill. Two of your most important jobs as an athlete are to contribute to the best of your ability and to appreciate the efforts of your teammates. A star player can't win without his team. The best teams recognize the less obvious talents of all their members and make the most of them.

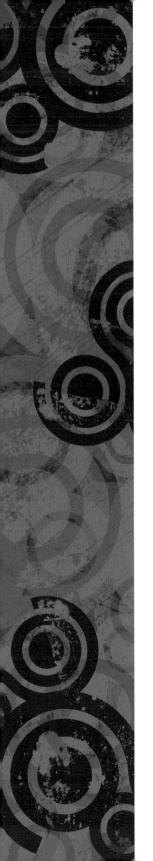

9

Extra Coaching

Youth sports would not exist without parents of some of the players handling many of the volunteer tasks. The majority of youth sports teams, particularly on the recreation level, are coached by a parent.

Having your parent as a coach immediately puts you on a different level than the other players. Your parent can't help wanting to see you succeed. The situation gets tricky if other players or parents suspect that the coach is giving you preferential treatment. As Marco learned, it can be difficult to convince other people that having a coach who is also your parent isn't always an advantage.

Marco's Story

Marco heard the whispers from other players in his weekend soccer league and even from their parents. "He only plays as much as he does because his father is coach." That's what they all seemed to be saying.

Marco did not think it was true, but it hurt to hear it anyway. In other sports, when his father was not coaching, Marco was one of the best players. He really thought that if his dad weren't the coach, he'd still be playing the same. Why couldn't others see it that way?

Before the season had started, Marco and his father had sat down to talk about what it would be like for Marco's father to be the coach.

Having your parent as a coach immediately puts you on a different level than the other players.

"Whether it's fair or not," Marco's dad had warned, "I have to demand more from you than everyone else, or else they'll think I'm playing favorites."

"Yeah, Dad," Marco had replied. "I think I understand."

"I'm really happy that I'll get to be your coach, Marco," his dad had continued. "I know that sometimes having your dad as coach is not as much fun as it should be, but I hope we'll have some really good times."

Think About It

- Have you played on a team where a parent of one of the players is the coach? Do you think the coach's kid was treated differently than the other players?

- Has your parent ever coached one of your teams? What was it like?

Remembering the conversation with his dad about not playing favorites, Marco was really upset when he heard the other parents accusing his dad of giving Marco extra attention. After a game, Marco heard Mr. Rice tell the other parents, "Any parent I've ever known who coached his kid's team made sure his kid got taken care of first. Why else would you do it?"

Baseball season came around and Marco started hearing the same types of comments again. Only this time, his father was no longer coaching. Julio's father was coaching for the first time. Marco really liked the way he demonstrated and explained everything about the game.

It was clear that Julio's father knew a lot about baseball. It was also clear that he had taught a lot of what he knew to Julio.

When the team played its first game, Julio was the shortstop. He made an error and his father called

him aside to go over the play. Marco saw teammates talking on the end of the bench and worried what they might be saying.

Julio pitched the second game. That's when the complaints started. Teammates started whispering that Julio got to play the most important positions because his father was in charge.

Think About It

- Do you think Marco or Julio got preferential treatment because their fathers were coaches?

- Have you ever thought that one of your teammates got extra playing time he didn't deserve? Did anybody say or do anything about it?

Marco decided he couldn't take it anymore. He called aside several of the teammates who were talking about Julio and his father.

"It's not fair to treat a teammate like that," he argued.

"Well, it's not fair that he can just ask his dad to play whatever position he wants," Derek responded.

Marco disagreed. "Julio's one of the best players on the team. Besides, I like his dad. I'm learning tons about baseball from him."

As he walked away, Marco was not sure what his teammates thought. He hoped they would think about what he said and realize he was right. Either way, he was proud of himself for sticking up for Julio's dad. He wished somebody had done the same for his father.

Think About It

- Do you agree with Marco that Julio deserves his position on the team? Why or why not?

- What could Marco and Julio's dads have done differently to make it clear they weren't playing favorites with their sons?

It's difficult to know exactly how to interact with your parent when he or she is also your coach. A coach-player relationship adds a new dimension to the parent-son relationship you already had, and sometimes finding the boundaries of this new relationship can be tricky. When can your parent treat you like a son, and when does your parent have to treat you as just another team member?

If one of your parents coaches your team, try to be aware that people might think you are receiving extra playing time or other favors. Sometimes you might end up taking extra laps or doing more work than the others just to prove you aren't getting special treatment. When someone else's parent is your coach, be thankful for the time they are spending with your team. Ask yourself: Is his or her son working hard? Is he a solid member of the team? Does he deserve the treatment he is receiving? Don't jump to conclusions that your coach is treating his or her own son differently from the rest of the team.

Work It Out

1. If one of your parents is going to be your coach, ask questions about how the team will be run.

2. Think about other parent-coaches you have worked with. Did their coaching relationships with their children work well? Try to model your behavior with your parent on other successful coach-child relationships you've seen.

3. You cannot stop other people's negative or jealous behaviors. Work hard, keep your head up, and focus on enjoying the game.

The Last Word from Tom

Playing on a team coached by one of your parents has the chance to be a special experience. It also has the chance to cause some truly uncomfortable moments. Teammates may be on the lookout for special treatment. Show your teammates you will try your hardest while not looking for any favors. It may not be easy to convince everyone, but if it's obvious you're just like anyone else on the team, you will likely be able to win them over. You can't control their perceptions, just your actions.

10

Which Sport to Choose?

When you're young, it's easy to play several sports. During the summer, it's no problem to have baseball on Saturdays and soccer on Wednesdays. It's also normal to play at least one sport each season in school. It's great to play a number of sports. Trying out a lot of different activities helps you learn what you enjoy and what you are good at.

When you get older, however, there may come a time when you want to concentrate on one sport only. There are good arguments for concentrating on fewer sports—how much more would you improve if you focused on training for one sport instead of multiple sports?

Some athletes face pressure when a coach from one sport competes against a coach from another sport for more of the athlete's time. Derek found what it was like to be asked to choose.

Derek's Story

Derek was good at every sport he played—baseball in the spring, soccer in the fall, and basketball in the winter. He had always loved sports, and he had always been good at everything he tried. Athletics just came naturally to him.

How much more would you improve if you focused on training for one sport?

Derek's parents gave him as many chances as possible to go to camps and clinics in the summer to learn more about each sport. Exposure at those camps led to invitations to go to more events. He was even invited to be on several all-star teams with the best players from his area.

Think About It

- Have you ever played multiple sports at the same time? How do you choose which sport or sports you want to play?

- What steps would you take if you wanted to get better at a sport?

Lately, Derek had started to hear the same message over and over. Each of his coaches wanted him to focus on that coach's sport alone.

Mr. Sosa called Derek over after a summer soccer workout.

"Good job today, Derek," he said. "I know you're going to the basketball tournament this weekend. But I really think you could be so much better at soccer if you got in more training. I think you could be looking at a scholarship someday. But you can't get there being a part-time player. If you gave up basketball, that extra time would make you unstoppable in soccer."

This was the same sales pitch he got when the club basketball coach wanted him to give up baseball so that he wouldn't have the layoff between his school and club seasons each year. And the baseball coach had pointed out that a little more batting cage time in the winter would make him into a better hitter early in the season.

Each coach made the same point: he'd never be as good as he could be if he devoted only some of his time to that coach's sport.

Think About It

- What factors might influence your decision to play many sports or concentrate on just one?

- How would you react to your coaches' pressure if you were in Derek's situation?

Derek opened his closet. He saw where each of his uniforms hung and the spot he had cleared out for any equipment he wasn't using. He thought about

the different sports. He wondered how each coach
could be sure that his sport was best for Derek. None
of them had seen him play the other sports much. It
occurred to Derek that their advice about his future
might have more to do with what was best for their
teams than with what was best for him as an athlete.

Derek sighed. He loved playing all of them, and
he didn't want to quit anything. He didn't want to
quit basketball not knowing if he could have been
good enough to play in college. But he couldn't
decide—what if not focusing on his swing in the off-
season meant he wouldn't reach his highest potential
in baseball?

Derek went out to the garage and found his
dad oiling a bike chain. "Dad," he began, "all of my
coaches want me to quit my other sports and focus
on one thing. I don't know what to pick."

"Do you like one sport more than the others?" his dad asked.

"No, I like them all the same. And I'm afraid I'll choose the wrong one."

Derek's dad gave him a measuring look. "You say all your coaches want you to choose?"

"Yeah."

"Well, I think that as long as you make the teams and keep up with your homework, there's no reason you have to quit any sports."

"They say I'll never be as good if I don't focus," Derek argued.

"Well, you won't be as good if you start to question what you're doing, either," his dad replied. "Let me know if your coaches give you any trouble, and I'll come talk to them with you. Okay?"

"Okay," said Derek. "Thanks, Dad." Derek felt better already.

Think About It

- If you had to choose among your activities, which do you think you would pick? Why?

- Do you think Derek's dad gave him good advice? What advice would you give Derek?

While it is true that concentrating on one sport might develop your skills faster, there are also benefits to learning a variety of skills. Learning to play several sports or several positions within a sport helps develop different skills and reduces the risk of burnout and injuries.

While some people would rather concentrate on one activity all the time, many people like to do a variety of things. Changing sports with the season can help keep all sports fun.

If a coach pressures you to play only one sport but you're not ready to specialize, it might help to talk things over with your parents. They will be your backup if you have to have a discussion with your coach about your decision to stay in several sports or choose to go with a different sport entirely.

Work It Out

1. Weigh the pros and cons of playing several sports versus concentrating on one sport. Remember, it's not just about what you are good at but also what you enjoy. It might help to talk this out with your parents or another trusted adult, too.

2. Don't worry about specializing too soon. Eventually, you'll discover if you have greater skill or interest in one sport over another.

3. If you feel a coach is pressuring you, ask your parents or another trusted adult to help you discuss the situation with the coach. A good coach will support your best interests.

The Last Word from Tom

Do you picture yourself as someone who would be happier being part of several teams or being limited to one sport, but doing better at it? There is nothing wrong with either decision. You may eventually pick one sport. But there's no need to hurry that decision. Take the time to make the right choice and only choose when you know you are ready. You can always play some sports at a less competitive level. This can help you become a lifelong athlete.

My first experience participating in sports was playing football in a program my own father created. Through the years, he showed me the way in many sports. He taught me my golf swing, how to block the ball as a catcher, and how to check the field the same way every time as a quarterback. Most important, he taught me about fair play, good sportsmanship, and teamwork.

The variety of my experiences in youth and high school sports came not only from trying different activities but also from doing them in different settings—first in a small town where a position on a team was practically a given, then in a midsize city where it was necessary to fight for every spot.

I learned there are benefits to being the central player on a team and also supporting others in the smallest role. You can celebrate small successes during a losing season or rejoice as the last seconds tick down during the championship game to your victory. And you can learn from every one of these experiences.

There are many potential conflicts that can sidetrack us along the way. If we can manage those situations, however, there is also a lifetime full of memories to be shared with friends and family.

So, play ball!

Tom

Remember, a healthful life is about balance. Now that you know how to walk that path, pay it forward to a friend or even yourself! Remember the Work It Out tips throughout this book, and then take these steps to get healthy and get going.

- If you hope to play on a higher-level team some day, go watch them play. Study how it is different from the level you currently play at. Try to determine what you will have to improve on before moving to that level.

- Think about times when you have come away from a tough loss feeling respect for the opponent who just beat you or your team. Try to repeat some of those actions when you are on the winning side.

- Sports are goal oriented and often measured in numbers. Don't forget to concentrate on the process of how and why you are doing something.

- If you reach the point where you think it may be time to give up an activity, take your time and make a good decision. Be sure you feel ready for a change over a period of time rather than just during one bad week.

- While figuring out ways to improve yourself and your status on a team, also remember to think about what you can do on and off the field to make your team better.

- At the beginning of each new season, take time to think about why you are playing and what you hope to accomplish. When the season is over, compare how it went to what your goals were in the beginning.

- If your parents are involved in your sport, discuss with them what challenges may be ahead and how you will deal with them.

- Be willing to try other positions, not just other sports. By playing another position, you may find something else you are good at. If not, it is still helpful to develop a better understanding of what your teammates' responsibilities are.

Additional Resources

Selected Bibliography

Egendorf, Laura K. *Performance-Enhancing Drugs*. San Diego: Referencepoint Press, 2007.

"Know Your Role." *Through a Child's Eyes; A Parents' Guide to Improving Youth Sports*. 3 Jan. 2008. <http://www.sportsmanship.org/News/CTSA_PGuide_Final.pdf>.

Sheehy, Harry, and Danny Peavy. *Raising a Team Player: Teaching Kids Lasting Values on the Field, on the Court, and on the Bench*. North Adams, MA: Storey Publishing, 2002.

"Taking performance-enhancing drugs: Are you risking your health?" *MayoClinic.com*. 27 March 2008 <http://www.mayoclinic.com/health/performance-enhancing-drugs/HQ01105>.

"What About Sport Specialization?" *Through a Child's Eyes; A Parents' Guide to Improving Youth Sports*. 3 Jan. 2008. <http://www.sportsmanship.org/News/CTSA_PGuide_Final.pdf>.

Further Reading

McDaniels, Pellon. *So You Want to Be a Pro?* Lenexa, KS: Addax Publishing, 2002.

Robinson, Tom. *Performance-Enhancing Drugs*. Edina, MN: ABDO Publishing Company, 2009.

Robinson, Tom. *Sportsmanship in Youth Athletics*. Edina, MN: ABDO Publishing Company, 2009.

Web Sites

To learn more about handling sports, visit ABDO Publishing Company online at **www.abdopublishing.com**. Web sites about handling sports are featured on our Book Links page. These links are routinely monitored and updated to provide the most current information available.

For More Information

For more information on this subject, contact or visit the following organizations:

Citizenship Through Sports Alliance
2537 Madison Avenue, Kansas City, MO 64108
816-474-7264
www.sportsmanship.org
This coalition of professional and amateur sports organizations promotes fair play at all levels and strives to reinforce the value of sports as a test of character.

National Alliance for Youth Sports
2050 Vista Parkway, West Palm Beach, FL 33411
561-864-1141 or 800-688-KIDS
www.nays.org
This nonprofit organization advocates for positive and safe sports and activities for children. It provides services and resources for administrators, volunteer coaches, parents, officials, and young athletes.

Glossary

all-star
> A player who is selected as one of the best from his or her league.

athlete
> A person who participates in exercise, sports, or games requiring agility, strength, or stamina.

bench
> Where extra players sit during a game; also, the players who make up that group.

coach
> A person who instructs and makes decisions for a sports team.

official
> A person who administers the rules of a sports league or an individual contest. Also known as a referee or, in some sports, an umpire.

practice
> Working at a skill repeatedly in an attempt to become more proficient.

showboating
> Showing off while competing.

sports
> Physical activities or competitions engaged in for diversion or recreation.

sportsmanship

Fair, respectful, and gracious conduct while competing in sports and games.

taunting

Actions directed at an opponent to make him or her feel bad during competition.

teamwork

Members of a sports team working together toward a goal.

tryout

A practice session where players show their skills to try to make it onto a sports team.

Index

About the Author

Tom Robinson is a former newspaper sportswriter and sports editor who has written more than 20 books for young readers. His story on the use of expense money in the Pennsylvania Interscholastic Athletic Association was named one of the top ten news stories of 1998 in the 50,000–175,000 newspaper circulation category by the Associated Press Sports Editors. He lives with his family in Clarks Summit, Pennsylvania, where he has coached four sports on the youth level and one on the high school level.

Photo Credits

iStockphoto, cover, 3, 17, 44, 52; Shutterstock Images, 13, 25, 37, 61, 89; Bigstock, 18; Igor Stepovik/ Shutterstock Images, 28; Sylvain Legare/Shutterstock Images, 33; Carmen Martínez Banús/iStockphoto, 42; Pavel Losevsky/Fotolia, 51; Cynthia Farmer/Shutterstock Images, 58; Svetlana Atenzon/iStockphoto, 63; Katherine Welles/Shutterstock Images, 67; Fotolia, 71; Lorelyn Medina/Fotolia, 73; Nicholas Moore/Shutterstock Images, 79; Alistair Michael Thomas/Shutterstock Images, 81; Matthew Brown/iStockphoto, 82; Brent Reeves/Shutterstock Images, 91; Peter Kim/Shutterstock Images, 95; Jeff Thrower/Shutterstock Images, 97; Thomas Perkins/Fotolia, 98